Tim Deacon

93/200

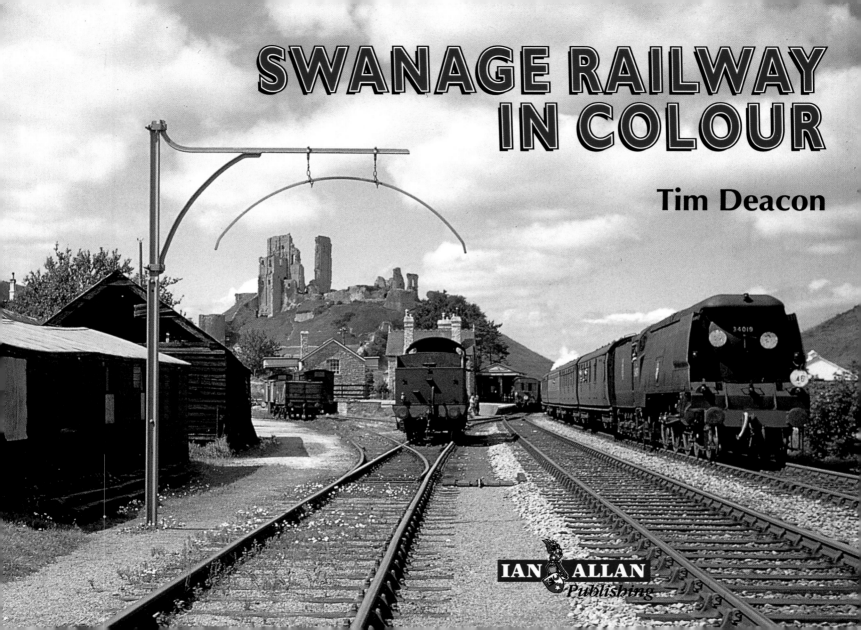

SWANAGE RAILWAY IN COLOUR

Tim Deacon

IAN ALLAN Publishing

First published 1996

ISBN 0 7110 2461 8

Published by Ian Allan Publishing

an imprint of Ian Allan Ltd, Terminal House, Station Approach, Shepperton, Surrey TW17 8AS. Printed by Ian Allan Printing Ltd, Coombelands House, Coombelands Lane, Addlestone, Surrey KT15 1HY.

Dedicated to all the long-serving and unflinching volunteers.

INTRODUCTION

Few, if any, railways in Britain can have a landmark of such significance as that of the Swanage branch line. From rail or road as you cross the Isle of Purbeck to Swanage you must pass Corfe Castle. The significance of this medieval structure became that much greater in August 1995 when, after almost 20 years' work, the Swanage Railway Project finally opened its long awaited extension from Harman's Cross to Corfe Castle and Norden. Like a medieval battle, the railway's volunteers had defeated a proposal to build a bypass on the trackbed, overcome local objections and finally conquered a near financial catastrophe that threatened to destroy all that had been achieved. As the first passenger-carrying train steamed into Corfe Castle station on that Saturday morning, all the hours of untold work and commitment by hundreds of unpaid volunteers melted away in the realisation of their success.

With the clock having been turned back over 30 years to the halcyon days of the branchline when steam-hauled trains passed the castle unnoticed many times a day, it was clear the objectives of the founding members of the Swanage Railway were achievable. There now remains just one and a half miles of overgrown trackbed between Norden and Railtrack's railhead at Furzebrook. With all royalties and profits from this book going to the final extension fund, we can only hope it will not be too long before a train can again depart from Swanage for Wareham.

After the publication of several first class books on the Swanage branchline it became clear that something was missing from them all — colour. All our memories of the line are in colour but all the books contain but a very few colour photographs. It is hoped to correct that imbalance with this volume of pre-preservation colour views of the complete length of the branch and its mainline interchange at Wareham. Along the way we will visit the Fayle's Tramway which brought much traffic to the branch.

A BRIEF HISTORY OF THE SWANAGE BRANCHLINE

As early as 1847 a scheme was put forward to build a branchline from Wareham, on the Southampton to Dorchester line, to serve the stone industry of Langton and Worth Matravers. The proposal met with strong opposition from the people of Wareham, landowners along the proposed route, and God-fearing folk, who saw the steam engine as an incarnation of the devil. Fourteen years were to pass before the London & Southern Western Railway put forward another proposal for a branch to serve the clay workings around Furzebrook and Norden. Again the people of Wareham strongly objected to the plan which would have involved breaching their Saxon walls, as they had when the Southampton to Dorchester line was proposed and which accounts for the station being so far from the town centre. The powerful and rich landowners still objected on various grounds and the scheme was stillborn. These same individuals, who also owned or had a controlling interest in the clay workings, had already constructed narrow gauge tramways to move their produce to the wharfs at Ridge, Slepe and Goathorn via the Pikes, Middlebere and Fayle's tramways.

A third proposal was put forward in 1862 by the Isle of Purbeck Railway Co and had the support of the LSWR. Yet again similar objections were forthcoming. The Parliamentary Bill of 22 June 1863 had to include a clause to please the burghers of Wareham, in so

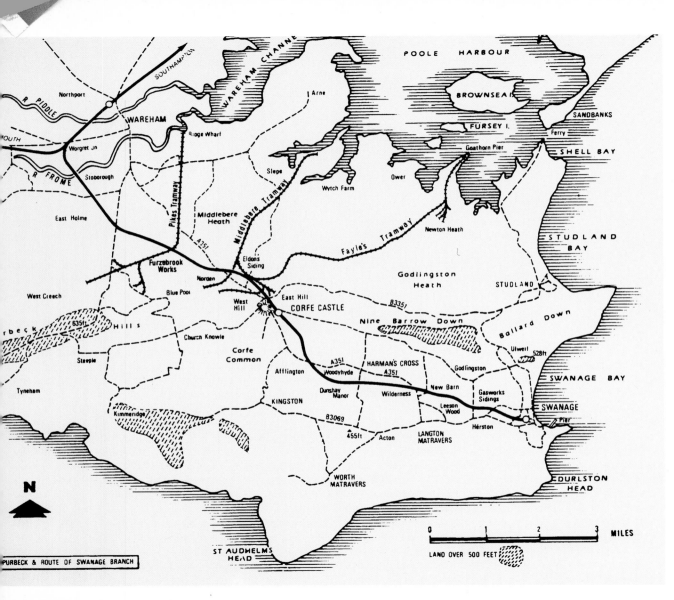

Front cover:
CORFE CASTLE STATION.
Storm clouds gather as weeds
grow in the disused goods yard
and steam has less than a month
left on local trains. Ivatt '2MT'
2-6-2T No 41316 hopes to out-
run the storm on its way to
Swanage in August 1966.
L. Golden

Back cover:
SWANAGE ENGINE SHED.
BR '4MT' 4-6-0 No 75079 is
well into its stride as it passes
the engine shed at Swanage and
crosses the stream by the
playing field. Note what are
now classic 1960s cars in the
field. Chris Phillips was lucky in
being able to 'reach the parts
other photographers could not'
at this time. In September 1965
this privilege was put to good
use after climbing up the
advanced starter signal with this
unusual but very interesting
view of an Eastleigh-bound
train. *C. Phillips*

PURBECK & ROUTE OF SWANAGE BRANCH

N

0   1   2   3   MILES

LAND OVER 500 FEET

much as a new station to the south of the town had to be constructed along with freight-exchange facilities by the wharfs on the River Frome. Further problems delayed construction and the Bill lapsed in 1868. Unperturbed, a further attempt was made in 1877 with the objectives of not only serving the clay and stone industries but also the growing popularity of Swanage as a fashionable new watering hole. The scheme had the backing of local entrepreneur George Burt and again the LSWR were only too keen to exploit the substantial potential of a line through the Purbecks. This time a new route was proposed that avoided the walls of Wareham by commencing some one and a half miles to the west of Wareham at Worgret, running via East Holme, Creech Bottom, Furzebrook and Norden then on to Corfe Castle and Swanage. Still there were objections and negotiations which would

take some four years before the granting of a Bill of Parliament in July 1881. With £90,000 worth of £10 shares raised and a further £30,000 in loans available, construction could commence.

BUILDING THE BRANCH

The Swanage Railway Act, 1881 authorised the construction of two railways: one from Worgret to Swanage via Corfe Castle and the other from Swanage station to the Mowlem Institute, connecting with the narrow gauge tramway round to the pier purely for the movement of stone. This second line was never constructed and the land became Commercial Road at the back of Station Road. No provision was made in the Act for sidings at Furzebrook or Norden, these being laid at later dates and financed by the customers and the LSWR.

Responsibility for the construction of the branch was split between the Swanage Railway Co and the LSWR. George Burt contracted Messrs Galbraith and Church to survey a route and draw up specifications and plans. Five companies then tendered for the contract to construct the 10-mile line and two stations, two goods sheds and an engine shed. Tenders ranged from £76,646 to £92,995, the Swanage Railway Co having budgeted for £77,000 excluding the track. Also included in this figure were 29 bridges, culverts and three viaducts. The successful contractor was Curry & Reeves of Westminster, with E. G. Perkins of Lymington sub-contracted to build the two iron viaducts over the River Frome, the viaduct at Corfe Castle and the line from Worgret to Corfe Castle. The buildings at Corfe Castle and Swanage were constructed by Bull & Co of Southampton from Purbeck stone. Work commenced on 5 May 1883 and was completed by 20 May 1885 when the first passenger train departed from Swanage. Freight traffic started to use the line on the 1 June. The work was completed to date and within budget.

LOCOMOTIVES AND SERVICES

Though financed by the Swanage Railway Co, the branch was run from day one by the London & South Western Railway. As a result all classes of LSWR locomotives used on the main line would see service on the branch over the years, as long as they did not exceed the axle loading limitations. Best known and longest serving of the LSWR classes were the 'M7' 0-4-4Ts being used for some 40 years with two-coach push-pull sets, plus the occasional extra coach or two from mainline trains added at Wareham. The last 'M7', No 30107, ran on Saturday 9 May 1964. Most common on freight trains just after World War 2 were LSWR Class 700 'Black Motors' and SR 'Q' class 0-6-0s. By the early 1960s these were being replaced by BR Class 4MT 2-6-0s and 4MT 2-6-4Ts. Most classes of Southern Railway and British Railway Standard designs would see service on the branch, with the exception of Bulleid's 'Merchant Navy' class and BR 'Britannia' and '9F' designs. After the withdrawal of the 'M7s' and most other older Southern

PURBECK TRAMWAYS

NAME	PERIOD	TOTAL LENGTH	GAUGE
Pikes Tramway	1866-1957	5½ miles	2ft 8in
Fayle's Tramway	1905-1972	5⅓ miles	3ft 9in
	Rebuilt late 1940s		1ft 11in
Middlebere Tramway	1806-1905	3½ miles	2ft 8in
Newton Tramway	1868-n/a	1 mile	3ft 9in
Brownsea Island Tramway	1850-1878	½ mile	Unknown
Swanage Pier Tramway	1860-1932	⅓ mile	2ft 6in
Kimmeridge Shale Tramway	1848-1906	Unknown	Unknown
Cocknowle Tramway	1870-n/a	150yd	Unknown

Above:
WAREHAM STATION.
BR Brush Type 4 diesel-electric, now Class 47, No D1922 is pictured on a Weymouth-Waterloo express in the pouring rain during the summer of 1967. Note some of the many features that made Wareham such an interesting station in those days. *C. Phillips*

Freight traffic was more varied than on most Southern branch lines and was of course one reason why the line was constructed, with clay, stone and agricultural produce going out and coal, fertilizer and general goods coming in. Freight services to Corfe Castle and Swanage ceased on 4 October 1965. The only remaining freight traffic was ball clay from Furzebrook, which lasted until 1984 (with a siding still *in situ*, this traffic may resume in the future) by which time BP had built its rail facilities at Furzebrook.

The pre-World War 2 passenger timetable would resume in 1946 with 12 trains each way, including through workings. On summer Saturdays there were three through workings in each direction. On Sundays there would be six trips each way on the branch and through workings to Eastleigh plus odd excursions. The timetable appears to have altered little over the years. Troop specials and excursions from as far afield as the Midlands, Bristol and Bath working via the S&DJR were not unknown. This traffic diminished over the years but ramblers' specials continued until 1971. Closure of the branch was to be on the first day of 1972, the line's 87th year. Three-car Hampshire DEMU No 1110 was rostered for this duty along with No 1124 for the final trip.

locomotives, branchline trains were in the hands of Ivatt LMS '2MT' 2-6-2T and BR Standard '3MT' and '4MT' classes. The last regular steam locomotive on the branch was BR Class 4MT 2-6-0 No 76010 on 4 September 1966, though steam did cover for failed DEMUs over the next nine months. The following day three-car Hampshire DEMU No 1104 was to be the first of its class to see service on the branch. Other diesels were in use by the summer of 1966, though most through workings from Waterloo were still steam-hauled; Brush Type 4s and Crompton Type 3s would take over through services. Electro-diesels (of Classes 73 and 74) were to be seen firstly on permanent way and then tracklifting trains, removing three of the sidings at Swanage in early 1966. The remaining sidings and all other track, other than a single line to the main platform, had been lifted by early 1968.

TRAFFIC FIGURES FOR 1953

Local Passengers	131,494
Freight to	2,472*
Freight off	60,425*
Passengers to	102,646
Passengers off	101,444
Coal to	11,976*
Parcels to	9,939
Parcels off	28,711
(* In tonnes)	

POSTWAR STAFF ON THE BRANCH

Bill Langford — Line Manager; Frank Walden — Swanage and Corfe Castle Station Master; Jack Cannons — Swanage Station Foreman; Bill 'Taffy' Hazell — Swanage Porter; George Sims — Swanage Porter/Shunter; Albert Weekes — Swanage Porter; Ernie Farwell — Swanage Porter/Shunter; Tom Tetley — Swanage Porter/Shunter; Maurice Walton — Swanage Booking Clerk; Bryan Green — Swanage and Corfe Booking Clerk; Jimmy Hunt — Swanage and Corfe Signalman; Arthur Galton — Swanage and Corfe Signalman; Bob Richards — Swanage Porter/Shunter, Corfe Signalman; Bob Innes — Corfe Signalman; Ernie Peters — Corfe Porter/Signalman; Frank Kitcatt — Relief Signalman; Walter Burden — 1950 Worgret — Corfe P. W. Gang; Ken Andrews — 1950 Worgret — Corfe P. W. Gang; Sid Strichland — 1950 Worgret — Corfe P. W. Gang; Alfie Allingham — 1950 Worgret — Corfe P. W. Gang; Tony Trood — Last Swanage Branch P. W. Gang; Stan Smith — Last Swanage Branch P. W. Gang; Edwin 'Ted' Talbot — Last Swanage Branch P. W. Gang; Eddy Bird — Last Swanage Branch P. W. Gang; Cyril Tilly — Last Swanage Branch P. W. Gang; Charlie Bird — Last Swanage Branch P. W. Gang; John Coogan — Last Swanage Branch P. W. Gang; Arthur Stockley — Last Swanage Branch P. W. Gang; Tom Stockley — Last Swanage Branch P. W. Gang; Ken Rideout — Last Swanage Branch P. W. Gang; Tom Biles — Last Swanage Branch P. W. Gang; Peter Buglar — Guard; Alec Dudley — Guard; Stan Symes — Driver; Jack Hapgood — Driver; Doug Robinson — Fireman; Jack Spicer — Driver; Keith Sloper — Fireman; Johnny Walker — Driver; Stan Brown — Fireman; Ken Hordle — Driver; Bob Mitchell — Driver; Ted Viney - Fireman; Fred Norman — Fireman; Frank Farwell — Fireman; Mr Boyland — Driver; Nobby Boyland — Swanage Night Stoker; Eddie Brown — Worgret Signalman; Cliff Brown — Worgret Signalman

ACKNOWLEDGEMENTS

I would like to thank the following people for their contributions to this book: Colin Caddy, Michele and David Cook, Michael Gates, Laurie Golden, Duncan Gomersall, Bryan Green, David Haysom, George Moon, Julien Parker, Chris Phillips, David Pool, Anthony Storey, Barry Thirlwall, Martyn Thresh, Tony Trood, Mike Walshaw, Ron White of Colour-Rail, Andrew P. M. Wright.

Below:
WAREHAM STATION. BR Class 4MT 2-6-0 No 76010 has just arrived with a train from Swanage. No 76010 will now run round its train before shunting it into the down bay platform to await its return trip to Swanage. With only one further day of steam-hauled local passenger services on the branch, Bournemouth MPD managed to find the filthiest locomotive they could for the occasion, Saturday 3 September 1966. *C. Phillips*

Right:
WAREHAM STATION.
On the last day of branchline services Hampshire Class 3H DEMU (diesel-electric multiple-unit) No 1110 waits in the down bay platform for passengers from a Weymouth train. Class 33/2 'Cromptons' were employed for some 20 years, before the Bournemouth-Weymouth line was electrified, hauling electric stock. On Saturday 1 January 1972 No 6531 is seen beside the old water column. *B. Thirlwall*

Left:
WAREHAM STATION.
After working a weedkiller train down the Swanage branch on Monday 16 May 1966, BR Class 4MT 2-6-0 No 76026 is seen taking water before proceeding to its next destination. Note the inscription on the tender, S&DJR (Somerset & Dorset Joint Railway). *G. Moon*

Right:
WORGRET JUNCTION.
A BR Class 4MT 2-6-0 No.76014 on a Furzebrook clay empties train collects the single line token from the Worgret junction signalman. This train would spend some time on the branch shunting at the Pike Bros china clay sidings at Furzebrook, before returning with the loaded wagons. By this date, Tuesday 7 June 1966, this was the only freight traffic using the branch after the closure of Corfe Castle and Swanage goods yards on 4 October 1965. *M. H. Walshaw*

Left:

WORGRET JUNCTION.
Another view of a train collecting a token from the Worgret junction
signalman, Eddie Brown. This time it is an Ivatt '2MT' 2-6-2T on a
Swanage train. The token will be given up at Corfe Castle in
exchange for a Corfe-Swanage tablet, on Thursday 9 September 1965.
M. H. Walshaw

Above:

RIVER FROME VIADUCTS.
A Wareham-bound train crosses the River Frome headed by an Ivatt
'2MT' 2-6-2T in August 1966. The two iron viaducts over the River
Frome were constructed as part of a sub-contract undertaken by
E. G. Perkins of Lymington in 1884. *L. Golden*

Left:
EAST HOLME.
A Swanage-bound train is about to pass under a minor road bridge at East Holme. Ivatt '2MT' 2-6-2T No 41316 is seen on the long straight stretch from the River Frome viaducts in August 1965.
C. L. Caddy

Above:
EAST HOLME.
Moving to the other side of the road bridge used for the previous view, we see Bulleid 'West Country' No 34023 *Blackmore Vale* (now preserved on the Bluebell Railway) on the LCGB 'Dorset Coast Express' special. On the rear of this train was BR '4MT' 2-6-4T No 80011, which hauled the train back to Wareham. Note how the bridge and trackbed had been built with the foresight of the possible need for double track. The date is Sunday 7 May 1967. *C. L. Caddy*

Right:
FURZEBROOK.
BR '4MT' 2-6-4T No 80094 is seen shunting empty china clay wagons for the loading dock of Pike Bros on Monday 2 May 1966. In the background can be seen the loaded wagons waiting to be coupled to the brakevan directly in front of the locomotive. How this location has changed today; the clay siding still remains, out of use at the present, but to the left of this view is now the Wytch Farm oilfield storage and distribution siding. *Colour-Rail*

Opposite:
CORFE CASTLE VIADUCT.
Class M7 0-4-4T No 30111, with the wind behind it, heads away from Corfe Castle viaduct with a Maunsell push-pull set in September 1963. This scene can once more be witnessed with the Swanage Railway's preserved 'M7', No 30053, purchased from Steamtown (Pennsylvania, United States of America) in 1987, and a restored push-pull set. *A. Storey*

Above:
CORFE CASTLE STATION.
A broadside view of LSWR '700' class 0-6-0 No 30695, seen across the public house gardens, whilst in the down platform on shunting manoeuvres during the summer of 1961. This class was the backbone of freight haulage on the branch for many years after World War 2. The class was replaced in the early 1960s by Southern Railway 'Q' class 0-6-0s. *Colour-Rail*

Right:
CORFE CASTLE STATION.
BR Class 3MT No 82027 waits with a Wareham-bound train as Ivatt '2MT' No 41314 drifts in with a Swanage train on Monday 18 May 1964, just nine days after the last 'M7' passed through the station.
M. Gates

Right:
CORFE CASTLE STATION.
The LCGB 'Dorset Coast
Express' special of 7 May 1967
had a locomotive at either end
on each run down the branch.
Hauled down by Bulleid 'West
Country' No 34023 *Blackmore
Vale*, the first return trip was
headed by BR '4MT' 2-6-4T
No 80011, seen here in close-up
at the north end of the station.
M. Gates

Opposite:
CORFE CASTLE STATION.
A superb panoramic view of
Corfe Castle station as a
London-bound summer Saturday
through service gets right of
way. The smoke from the
Type 3's exhaust can be seen as
it gets a rake of '3TC' and
'4TC' EMUs moving on 22 July
1967. In the background can be
seen one of the two Pullman
camping coaches, the last of a
number of different coaches
used for this purpose over the
years. These two would end
their days being burnt and cut
up on site. *C. L. Caddy*

Right:
CORFE CASTLE STATION.
One might say that this was the
perfect picture of Corfe Castle
station. This view was taken in
August 1956. With the castle
framed within the loading gauge,
Bulleid 'West Country'
No 34019 *Bideford* departs for
Swanage with a through train
from Waterloo. In the up
platform is a Wareham-bound
local and in the goods yard
ex-SECR 'N' class 2-6-0 waits
light engine. *Colour-Rail*

Left:
CORFE CASTLE STATION.
Just before Christmas 1965 Ivatt
'2MT' 2-6-2T No 41230 waits
to depart for Swanage. Plenty of
steam to spare for coach
heating, we hope. *C. L. Caddy*

Right:
SOUTH OF CORFE CASTLE.
Ivatt '2MT' 2-6-2T No 41316 is
seen heading south from Corfe
Castle on a local train. The
locomotive is about to pass
under the A351 road bridge in
August 1965. *C. L. Caddy*

Above:

HARMAN'S CROSS.
Ivatt '2MT' 2-6-2T No 41230 passes under Haycraft,s Lane bridge just south of Harman's Cross in August 1966. From December 1988 Swanage Railway operations ran as far as a newly constructed station just to the north of this road bridge. Since 12 August 1995 this station has become a passing point for trains to and from Corfe Castle and Norden. *L. Golden*

Right:

HERSTON.
On Saturday 18 June 1966 rebuilt Bulleid 'West Country' No 34012 *Launceston* is seen at the end of the long climb from Swanage station hauling the 11.20am (SO) Swanage-Waterloo service past the future location of Herston Halt. *D. E. Pool*

Above:
VICTORIA AVENUE ROAD BRIDGE.
That clean exhaust from Bulleid 'West Country' No 34040 *Crewkerne* conceals the hard work involved lifting its 8-coach 11.20am (SO) Swanage-Waterloo train up to the Victoria Avenue road bridge. On the date of this photograph, Saturday 26 June 1965, steam-hauled through services had only two years to go before total dieselisation of the branch. *D. E. Pool*

Right:
VICTORIA AVENUE ROAD BRIDGE.
A scene that the Swanage Railway has recreated since the restoration and return to service of 'M7' 0-4-4T No 30053 in June 1992. On Wednesday 6 September 1961 'M7' No 30108 is seen on the 5.38pm Swanage-Wareham train. *D. E. Pool*

Left:
SWANAGE ENGINE SHED.
Class M7 0-4-4T No 30060 is
seen arriving at Swanage with a
local train and crossing over to
the bay platform line. This
view in May 1957 depicts the
engine shed with its original
stone arch doorway; this
unfortunately was damaged in
1958 and the next view shows
the far less elegant resulting
repair. *Colour-Rail*

Right:
SWANAGE ENGINE SHED.
The new order: 'Crompton'
Type 3 Bo-Bo diesel-electric
No D6533 arrives with the
(SuO) Eastleigh-Swanage service
on Sunday 19 June 1966.
D. E. Pool

Above:

SWANAGE ENGINE SHED.
Rebuilt Bulleid 'West Country' No 34005 *Barnstaple* departs past the engine shed with an (SO) Swanage–Waterloo service. Considering the gradient and the load No 34005 is hauling, it is surprising to see the safety valve lifting so soon into the long climb out of Swanage.
C. Phillips

Right:

SWANAGE ENGINE SHED.
Rebuilt Bulleid 'West Country' No 34004 *Yeovil* passes the now disused engine shed, turntable and track into the goods yard and bay platform, whilst working the Warwickshire Railway Society tour from Birmingham. On the rear was BR '4MT' 2-6-4T No 80146 which hauled the train back to Wareham on Sunday 11 June 1967.
C. Phillips

Left:
SWANAGE ENGINE SHED.
The regular branch 'Q' class 0-6-0, No 30539, is seen on shed. After turning it will have taken on more water and, whilst the crew have their lunch, No 30539 takes a well-earned rest from shunting the goods yard on Thursday 17 August 1961. *G. Moon*

Above:
SWANAGE SIGNALBOX.
BR '4MT' 2-6-4T No 80134 is caught by the weak winter sun as it waits to set back on to its train in the bay platform during late 1965. *C. Phillips*

31

Left & above:
SWANAGE SIGNALBOX.
Two views of this distinctive and attractive signalbox that, hopefully, will be rebuilt one day by the Swanage Railway. Well-known Swanage signalman Jimmy Hunt can be seen in one view. Also note the superb condition in which the interior was kept. *C. Phillips*

Right:
SWANAGE SIGNALBOX.
Rebuilt Bulleid 'West Country' No 34044 *Woolacombe* is ready to depart for Waterloo with a summer Saturday through working. Note the green flag; due to the length of this train the signalman is unable to release the signal and the driver is therefore shown the green flag from the signalbox and verbally told he can safely depart. *C. Phillips*

Left:

SWANAGE SIGNALBOX.
In latter years double-headed trains on the branch were comparatively rare and were normally caused in summer by the need to get either the train locomotive from a through service from Waterloo or a pilot engine back to Bournemouth MPD. In this view we see Ivatt '2MT' 2-6-2T No 41314 double-heading a BR '4MT' 2-6-4T on a late Saturday afternoon train with the sun low in the sky. *C. Phillips*

Above:

SWANAGE SIGNALBOX.
An early visit of a Type 3 Crompton Bo–Bo (later to be known as Class 33) diesel-electric No D6533 sees the driver handing over the Corfe Castle-Swanage tablet to Arthur Galton, the Swanage signalman, in 1964.
B. Green

Left:

SWANAGE GOODS YARD.
This view shows just how large Swanage goods yard was. Here we see 'Q' class No 30539 preparing to leave with its freight train on Thursday 7 September 1961. From the goods yard coal was distributed to Swanage and the surrounding area. In addition, two stonemasons worked at opposite ends of the yard; one, based on the corner of Court Road, was known for his dinosaur footprints set in slabs of Purbeck stone. The 'Q' class replaced the long-serving LSWR '700' class 0-6-0s, better known as 'Black Motors', before itself being replaced by BR Standard classes. *D. E. Pool*

Above:

SWANAGE GOODS YARD.
On Saturday 27 August 1966, BR '4MT' 2-6-4T No 80019 was the Swanage pilot. It is seen here beside the disused dock in siding No 3. In the background can be seen the 11.20am (SO) Swanage-Waterloo train. Also on this day, sister Class 4MT No 80146 was working one of the local trains. *C. L. Caddy*

Above:
SWANAGE GOODS YARD.
Rebuilt Bulleid 'West Country' No 34040 *Crewkerne* arrives at Swanage with the 10.30am (SO) Waterloo-Swanage train in 1966. *C. Phillips*

Right:
SWANAGE GOODS YARD.
A BR Class 4MT 2-6-4T is seen drawing a long rake of empty coal wagons out of the goods yard on Tuesday 7 September 1965, less than a month before freight services ceased. *M. H. Walshaw*

Right:
SWANAGE STATION.
On Thursday 16 September 1971 Berkshire three-car DEMU No 1129 arrives at a dismal scene of decay and dereliction as Mother Nature begins to reclaim the station site. At least the setting sun shows what remains to best effect as the 17.57 from Wareham draws into the platform. *D. E. Pool*

Opposite:
SWANAGE STATION.
In happier days the classic 'M7' 0-4-4T No 30105 and push-pull set await departure on the 4.20pm to Wareham on Wednesday 26 September 1962. *J. D. Gomersall*

Opposite:
SWANAGE STATION.
Rebuilt Bulleid 'West Country'
No 34005 *Barnstaple* is in superb
condition as it awaits departure
for Waterloo. The driver
appears to be contemplating the
task ahead. *C. Phillips*

Left:
SWANAGE STATION.
A Western Region BR
Class 3MT 2-6-2T No 82004 is
seen drawing up to its train.
Believe it or not, under that
heavy covering of grime is a
green livery. No 82004 was at
that time to be found working
over the Somerset & Dorset
Joint line and was based at Bath
(Green Park) shed. A motive
power shortage at Bournemouth
in 1966 must have led to it
being borrowed for this service.
C. Phillips

Left:
SWANAGE STATION.
BR Class 4MT 2-6-0 No 76065 is unusually caught in a good light at
the buffer stops. This might be a (SuO) Eastleigh train judging by the
stock.
C. Phillips

Right:
SWANAGE STATION.
Another Class 4MT 2-6-0 is seen at the opposite end of the station
during the summer of 1966. Driver Jack Hapgood and guard Alec
Dudley are checking train details or perhaps a tip for the 3.20 at
Wincanton, who knows?
C. Phillips

Right:
SWANAGE STATION.
Two views of the rare sight of a Brush Type 4 diesel-electric (now Class 47) at Swanage. Visits were few and occurred only over a two-year period from mid-1965 to June 1967. These visits were with Waterloo or Eastleigh trains. No D1690 is shown waiting with a Sundays only Eastleigh train during August 1966 in almost ex-works condition. *C. Phillips*

Left:
SWANAGE STATION.
Brush diesel-electric No D1922, having arrived from Eastleigh with a (Sundays only) service, will soon run round its train. It was unusual to get good photographs from this location due to the poor light at this end of Swanage station. *C. Phillips*

Right:
SWANAGE STATION.
Ramblers' specials were a regular occurrence in the postwar years and would bring unusual locomotives to Swanage. The year 1971 was to see its fair share of such specials. In August 1971 three four-coach, Western Region diesel-mechanical multiple-units (DMUs) formed one such special. *C. Phillips*

Left:
SWANAGE STATION.
Rebuilt Bulleid 'West Country' No 34044 *Woolacombe*, with mostly
Midland Region stock, waits for the branch train to arrive. One
wonders what the driver, fireman and guard were all looking at — a
map? Driver to Fireman: 'We turn right at Worgret.' The guard is
not so sure! *C. Phillips*

Above:
SWANAGE STATION.
On the final day of British Railways services on the branch,
Hampshire Class 3H DEMU No 1110 waits to make one of the last
trips to Wareham on 1 January 1972. *B. Thirlwall*

49

FAYLE'S NARROW GAUGE TRAMWAY

Left:
FAYLE'S CORFE CASTLE.
A loaded train is pictured on
6 September 1965 heading for the
Norden interchange.
B. Thirlwall

Below:
FAYLE'S CORFE CASTLE.
4WDM Ruston Hornsby
No 391127 is seen on
16 September 1969 crossing the
A351 road with loaded wagons
for the Norden interchange. Clay
was transferred either to lorries at
Norden, just behind the recently
opened Swanage Railway station,
or taken to an exchange siding
just to the north. *B. Thirlwall*

Left:
SWANAGE STATION.
A once-a-year visit by the
weedkiller train is caught in the
station. The six old locomotive
tenders are of SECR origin and
the four SR luggage vans are
being put to a very different use
in this train on Monday 16 May
1966. *G. Moon*

Left:

SWANAGE ENGINE SHED.
A favourite location for photographers before and since preservation is Northbrook Road bridge. Here we see a train from the early days of the Swanage Railway. On Monday 31 August 1981 Hunslet 0-6-0ST No 1690 *Cunarder* is seen on the shuttle that worked half-way to the Victoria Avenue Road bridge at this time. In the background can be seen the Swanage Railways first steam locomotive Barclay, 0-4-0ST *Richard Trevithick. C. L. Caddy*

Above:

SWANAGE STATION.
 A special visiting locomotive, unrebuilt Bulleid 'West Country' No 34105 *Swanage*, is seen in the Swanage station loop on Saturday 20 March 1993. During the early years of the Swanage Railway project members had been competing with the Mid-Hants Railway to see who could raise the money to purchase this engine. Unfortunately, the Swanage Railway had to settle for No 34072 *257 Squadron*, a superb locomotive, but not the line's namesake. *C. L. Caddy*

Left:
SWANAGE STATION.
Freight traffic returns to Swanage; shame that the goods yard had become a car park and bus terminus. On 26 September 1992 Yugoslavian-built 0-6-0T No 30075 is seen with a demonstration freight train. *Andrew P. M. Wright*

Above:
NORTHBROOK ROAD BRIDGE.
Ex-LSWR T9 class 4-4-0 No 30120 is seen coming on shed under Northbrook Road bridge. Note the superb condition of this National Railway Museum locomotive whilst in the care of the Swanage Railway volunteers. *C. Phillips*

Above:

NORTHBROOK ROAD BRIDGE.
During 1994 the Swanage Railway was privileged to have the world's most famous steam locomotive *Flying Scotsman* present on the line. It is seen here passing under Northbrook Bridge and past No 34072 *257 Squadron* on its way to Harman's Cross. It is seen in BR livery and carrying its BR number of 60103 rather than its better known LNER number 4472. This visit gave a much-needed boost to the line's morale as volunteers strove to complete the extension to Corfe Castle and Norden. *C.Phillips*

Right:

CORFE CASTLE STATION.
On Saturday 12 August 1995 trains once more called at Corfe Castle station after 23 years. The very first passenger-carrying train has just arrived at Corfe Castle from Swanage hauled by ex-LSWR Class M7 0-4-4T No 30053. Driver Ron Roberts and fireman Steve Dyer will take this train on to the new station at Norden where Bulleid 'Battle of Britain' No 34072 *257 Squadron* was waiting for the return trip.
Andrew P. M. Wright

Above:
CORFE CASTLE STATION.
257 Squadron is seen entering Corfe Castle station from Norden during the first week of the new service. A classic view if only the train did not have to use the up platform in both directions due to the lack of a passenger footbridge at this time. *Andrew P. M. Wright*

Right:
CORFE CASTLE STATION.
After a pause of just two minutes *257 Squadron* is about to depart for Harman's Cross and Swanage. Let's hope that very soon trains from Wareham, and even London, will be departing from Corfe Castle for Swanage. *Andrew P. M. Wright*

S. R.
TRESPASSERS
WILL BE
PROSECUTED

Above:
CORFE CASTLE STATION.
Another Swanage-bound train arrives with a good head of steam; the safety valve is lifting as No 30053 drifts into the station with its four-coach train. *Andrew P. M. Wright*

Right:
CORFE CASTLE.
A different view of the station and castle with a very different train. During the long summer evenings that followed the opening of the extension, full use was made of the recently restored BR Derby Works-built Class 108 two-car DMU. *Andrew P. M. Wright*

Opposite:
NORDEN STATION.
On Sunday 19 November 1995 M7 0-4-4T No 30053 is seen arriving at the new station at Norden with the first train of the day. The bridge in the background used to carry the Fayle's narrow gauge line over the branch to an exchange siding nearby.
Andrew P. M. Wright

Left:
THE WAY AHEAD.
Looking towards Furzebrook and the remaining part of the branch owned by Railtrack and used by BP. No 30053 stands in the current headshunt at Norden, which soon will be part of the line to Furzebrook and Wareham. Thanks to the help of Operations Manager Roger Sinar and other members of staff No 30053 was specially turned to face Wareham just to get this symbolic picture, showing the way ahead for the Swanage Railway.
Andrew P. M. Wright

FURZEBROOK.

Just over a mile from the headshunt at Norden is the end of the Swanage branch currently used by gas trains. A very different Furzebrook in the 1990s compared to the picture of BR '4MT' No 80094 in May 1966. The Fayle Ball Clay company siding is still *in situ* but has been disused since 1984. The run round facility is used by the gas trains whilst shunting. In this view can be seen a BR Class 60 during shunting manoeuvres on Friday 30 August 1991.
Andrew P. M. Wright